*L*OOKING AT *P*AINTINGS

Landscapes

When the Mountains Meet the Mist, 1973
Diana Kan, American, born 1927

LOOKING AT PAINTINGS

Landscapes

Peggy Roalf

Series Editor
Jacques Lowe

Designer
Amy Hill

Hyperion Books for Children
New York

A
JACQUES LOWE
VISUAL ARTS PROJECTS
BOOK

Text © 1992 by Jacques Lowe Visual Arts Projects Inc.

A Jacques Lowe Visual Arts Projects Book

Printed in Italy

FIRST EDITION

1 3 5 7 9 10 8 6 4 2

LIBRARY OF CONGRESS CATALOGING-IN-PUBLICATION DATA
Roalf, Peggy.
Landscapes/Peggy Roalf—1st ed.
p. cm.—(Looking at paintings)
"A Jacques Lowe Visual Arts Projects Book"—T.p. verso
Includes bibliographical references and index.
Summary: An exploration of painting through 2000 years of art
history, focusing on paintings of landscapes by various artists.
ISBN 1-56282-303-5 (trade)—ISBN 1-56282-302-7 (lib. bdg.)
1. Landscape painting—History—Juvenile literature.
[1. Landscape in art. 2. Painting—History. 3. Art appreciation.]
I. Title. II. Series: Roalf, Peggy. Looking at Paintings.
ND1343.R6 1992
758'.1—dc20 92-52980
CIP
AC

Contents

To John Gundelfinger, with love

Introduction

LOOKING AT PAINTINGS is a series of books about understanding what great artists see when they paint. Painters have created landscapes — personal visions of the natural world — for thousands of years and for many different reasons.

Two thousand years ago, a Roman artist created landscape murals as decorations for extravagant country villas near Pompeii. These works of art depicted luxury, wealth, and tranquillity, all of which vanished with the eruption of Vesuvius. When they were unearthed by archaeologists in 1748, these murals, created by a forgotten painter, captured the public's imagination with their great beauty and artistry.

Until books became widely available in sixteenth-century Europe, most stories were told through paintings, and most landscapes were created as backgrounds in religious art. Joachim Patinir was so astonished by the world's vastness and beauty that, unlike his contemporaries, he made the landscape the most important subject of his work. In *Landscape with Saint Jerome,* the old scholar is the last thing we would notice in this enormous painting.

Before science provided explanations for natural occurrences, the world was not merely a place of beauty — it was also to be feared. In *View of Toledo,* El Greco depicted the forces of a great storm and its power to make people seem insignificant by comparison.

In the twentieth century, many artists used the landscape as a theme to express their preference of nature to technology. In *Gray Hills,* Georgia O'Keeffe portrayed mountains so ancient and protected from the workings of mankind that they appear as nature's monuments.

Great artists transform what they see into images that take us to other times and distant places. You, too, can learn to look from a great mountain peak — or watch the autumn leaves fall in a dense forest — and use your imagination to see like a painter.

GARDEN LANDSCAPE WITH BIRDS AND FOUNTAIN,
detail, 40–30 B.C.
Unknown Roman artist, fresco, about 72" high

Wealthy citizens of ancient Rome escaped the stress of city life in their luxurious country houses. The Roman villa was a retreat, a place to relax and entertain guests with lavish banquets. The villa was often a visual feast, its interior walls covered with mural paintings.

This intimate garden landscape seems so real, we feel that we could step past the gilded red column and sip water from the little fountain. The painter created an illusion of realistic space and light by framing the landscape with a trompe l'oeil column. *Trompe l'oeil* is a French term that means to trick the eye into believing that an object painted on a flat surface is real. The artist painted a pattern of golden grapevines swirling around the column to create the appearance of a round, solid shape. On the left side of the column, the shapes of the foliage are repeated in a dark red, giving the appearance of shading and solidity. The transparent white highlight streaking from the top to the bottom, resembling reflected light, completes the illusion.

Even though the perspective is not realistic, the illusion created by the column is so believable that we accept the space of the landscape.

The artist continues his deception by painting the landscape in colors that advance and recede. The cool, dark brown forms of the cave seem to go back in space, whereas the warm golden ocher face of the rocks appears to project forward. At the top, the pale azure sky behind a grape arbor recedes into the distance. The artist unified this simple composition by repeating the leaves and vines throughout. And around the mouth of the cavern, four songbirds draw us into this peaceful scene.

LANDSCAPE WITH SAINT JEROME, undated

Joachim Patinir, Flemish (about 1480–1524), oil on board, 29⅛" x 35⅞"

*J*oachim Patinir completed his art training in 1515 in Antwerp, Belgium, a thriving city that attracted many painters. Patinir soon became known as the first European landscape specialist: as an apprentice, he had created landscape backgrounds for other artists; later, as a master artist, he created sweeping panoramas that suggest the vastness of the earth. Although Patinir painted pictures with religious themes, the figures are always secondary to his grand vision of the earth.

Patinir imagined standing atop a high mountain to create this bird's-eye view across fields and valleys, over lakes and islands to a seemingly limitless horizon. By placing the line of the horizon near the top and varying the angle of view, he emphasized the depth of the space. At first, it seems that Patinir is looking down from a high place. But he painted the buildings, people, and animals straight on, from ground level. The subtle change in the point of view, from one wedge-shaped field to another, allows us to see and appreciate the variety of natural forms and architecture.

Patinir used only four basic colors—cool greens, silvery blues, golden ocher, and brown. By mixing delicate shades of each color, he unified the vast space of the landscape. Everything—from the flowers in the foreground to the island castles in the distance—is painted in almost microscopic detail. Patinir's superrealistic painting style creates a dream-like impression of the natural world.

To Patinir, human activity seemed unimportant compared to nature's immensity and variety.

VIEW OF ARCO, 1495
Albrecht Dürer, German (1471–1528), watercolor and body color on paper,
$8^{11}/_{16}"$ x $8^{11}/_{16}"$

*A*lbrecht Dürer was a painter who was inspired by the potential of the printing press to bring knowledge to a great number of people. He became famous in his lifetime as the illustrator, editor, and printer of books that circulated throughout Europe.

Dürer expanded his artistic vision by traveling whenever he could leave his busy workshop. In Venice, Italy, he visited Andrea Mantegna and Gentile Bellini and saw their landscape paintings. Like Joachim Patinir, these artists created fantastic landscapes as backgrounds for religious paintings. Because he enjoyed studying nature, Dürer began to create paintings in which natural scenery was the main subject.

Albrecht Dürer painted this exquisitely detailed watercolor to study natural forms. With this knowledge, he enriched the detail in his landscape paintings.

On his journey from Venice to his home in Nuremberg, Dürer painted this view of a fortified mountain village. He framed the picture with grayish brown rocks at the bottom and on the left to emphasize the massive hill. A curving road leads our eyes to Arco, but Dürer slows down our journey by painting the vineyards, olive groves, and a farmer in great detail. He shaped these precise details with a brush squeezed almost dry to form a sharp point.

Dürer mastered the art of perspective by adding opaque white paint to his cool transparent watercolors; for the background, he whitened the green and earthy brown slopes to create a hazy distance. Through the careful balance of stronger color and fine detail in the middle of the picture, and the pale, almost abstract background, Dürer combined his detailed observations with his personal vision of nature.

fenedier klawsen

13

THE ADORATION OF THE SHEPHERDS, detail, about 1505–10
Giorgione da Castelfranco, Italian (1475/7–1510), on panel, 35¾" x 43½"

Giorgione was inspired by the quality of the light in Castelfranco, the hill town where he was born. His keen observation of nature led him to create a new painting method that was revolutionary at the time.

In the sixteenth century, artists were taught to create detailed drawings and to study every aspect of their subject before painting. The masterful use of color was secondary to an artist's ability to draw. But Giorgione imagined his pictures in color, and he worked in color from the first stages. He had observed that outlines do not occur in nature; that the appearance of a solid form is shaped by sunlight and shade. Giorgione created an atmosphere of light, air, and space by building up gradual shades of color that were never trapped by lines.

Giorgione made this nativity scene seem like a contemporary event in the lives of real people by locating it in the countryside where he had lived as a child.

Giorgione takes us on a circular walk into the landscape through the use of curved shapes and vertical forms. He composed the lake with three flattened ovals that become smaller in size as they recede into the background. A little path arcs back from the shore toward the hillside beyond. The geometric contours of the golden tower, lakeside villa, and ruined castle follow the circular route of Giorgione's design from the foreground to the horizon. With touches of red, Giorgione warmed the golden tones in the landscape to capture the incandescent light of the Venetian countryside.

Giorgione's most famous pupil, Titian, learned his master's secrets so well that until recently, art historians could not determine which artist had created this painting.

14

HUNTERS IN THE SNOW, 1565
Pieter Brueghel, Flemish (1525/30–69), oil on panel, 46" x 63¾"

*a*t a time when most artists painted dreamlike landscapes filled with heroic figures, Pieter Brueghel created intimate pictures of ordinary Flemish people who made their living from the land. In this painting, one in a series depicting the four seasons, Brueghel captured the frozen world of winter in a scene that stretches for miles. At first, the distant landscape seems like bleak territory. A closer look shows us that Brueghel filled this painting with dozens of people skating, fishing, and working.

Three stately trees and three hunters with a pack of hounds lead our eye in a diagonal line to the jagged, distant mountains. Brueghel enclosed the foreground with steep-roofed cottages that guide our eyes down the snowy slope to the different activities below. We notice the bright red color of an apron and the two women skating on a frozen inlet. Our eye moves past a farmer carrying firewood across a little bridge, to the open fields beyond. Here, Brueghel divided the large pond into two smaller areas, with people fishing through the ice on one side and playing games on the other.

To emphasize the bitter chill of winter, Brueghel painted a dull, greenish blue sky that seems to hang in a heavy mass over the landscape. In contrast, the warm brick color of the cottages and the windblown fire make the day seem even colder. He unified the picture by repeating the color of the sky through-out—on the footprints in the snow, on the river that winds back into the hills, and in the neighboring village at the horizon.

With an eye for humorous detail, Brueghel enlivened this chilly scene. Behind the village church, eight people with buckets and ladders attempt to put out a chimney fire.

VIEW OF TOLEDO, about 1597
El Greco (Doménikos Theotokópoulos), Spanish, born in Crete (1541–1614),
oil on canvas, 47¾" x 42¾"

The painter who became known as The Greek—El Greco, in Spanish—wandered from his native Crete to Venice, to Rome, and then to Madrid in search of a patron who would purchase his paintings. In the capital of Spain, King Philip II rejected him as a court painter. The king thought El Greco's colors were too harsh and his painting style too crude. Finally, in Toledo, Spain, the artist found a patron. El Greco became an official painter for the Catholic church in 1577, and he lived in Toledo for the rest of his life.

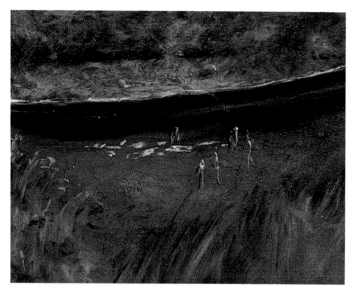

The antlike size of textile workers washing cloth in the river makes the landscape seem overwhelming.

This landscape painting was unusual for El Greco, who usually created religious paintings and portraits of church officials. El Greco captured the fury of a thunderstorm by exaggerating shapes and colors. He made the hill much steeper than it is in reality and perched the buildings precariously atop the cliff. Churning black clouds appear to be in motion, propelled by a fierce wind. The rocks and buildings seem to vibrate under the crackling white light that turns the color of the grass acid green. El Greco created an eerie contrast between the silvery cathedral and the sky by painting a band of menacing black clouds at the horizon.

With bold brushstrokes, El Greco formed the massive shapes of sky and land. He then added sharply defined highlights to the rocks, the trees, and the structures. By reversing the actual location of Toledo's cathedral and castle in this powerful landscape, El Greco focuses our attention on the church—his loyal patron for forty years.

EVENING: LANDSCAPE WITH AN AQUEDUCT, detail, 1818
Théodore Géricault, French (1791–1824), oil on canvas, 98½" x 86½"

Théodore Géricault began his career as a painter during a grim period in France's history: Napoléon had been defeated, and Paris was occupied by Russian and British soldiers. Géricault often symbolized his country's difficulties by depicting people faced with the destructive power of nature. His images of shipwrecks and drowning cause the viewer to identify with the fear of the people depicted in the painting. In this huge landscape painting, more than eight feet high, Géricault achieved the same kind of ominous effect.

Dangerously steep cliffs dominate this landscape. A ruined castle grows out of the hill. Atop a shadowy mountain we see the blank walls of a darkened tower. The aqueduct is like a fence blocking access to the lake beyond. Géricault stacked up one rocky form on top of another to create a fear-inspiring image.

Géricault painted a veil of shadows over most of this scene. First he painted the warm reddish brown colors of the landscape and the architecture. He then applied translucent layers of gray paint that allow the reddish brown to show through. By using a limited range of thinly painted colors, he created the haunting atmosphere of evening light.

In his short life, Géricault's awesome pictures of nature's power over people marked a change in a two-hundred-year-old French painting tradition. The same year that he created this landscape, Géricault won the gold medal at the most important art exhibition in Paris for his famous shipwreck painting, *The Raft of the Medusa.*

In this detail, tiny figures climbing and swimming help us to sense the enormous height of the cliffs.

ROAD WITH CYPRESS AND STAR, 1890
Vincent van Gogh, Dutch (1853–90), oil on canvas, 36¼" x 28¾"

In nature, Vincent van Gogh found the rhythm of his art. Every time he picked up a brush, he expressed his desire to bring joy to the people who saw his paintings. Van Gogh described this painting in a letter to his friend, the artist Paul Gauguin:

> I still have a cypress with a star from [Provence], a last attempt—a night sky with a moon without radiance, the slender crescent barely emerging from the opaque shadow cast by the earth—one star with an exaggerated brilliance, a soft brilliance of pink and green in the ultramarine sky, across which some clouds are hurrying. Below, a road bordered with tall yellow canes, an old inn with yellow lighted windows, and a very tall cypress, very straight, very somber. Very romantic, if you like, but also *Provence,* I think.

Van Gogh captured the pulsing flow of life itself with his powerful brushwork, using paint as thick as toothpaste. Each curving brush mark stands up from the canvas, allowing the colors underneath to show through. Individual strokes of yellow ocher, orange, ultramarine, and green, on top of cerulean blue, form a night sky that vibrates with light. Van Gogh repeated the green color that he used in the sky and in the cypress tree throughout—on the wavy surface of the road, among the flamelike stalks of cane, and on the little inn. With dashes of white paint, he bathed the landscape in the ghostly light of a lunar eclipse.

Vincent van Gogh's fragile mental health collapsed two months after he created this landscape, and he took his own life. His passion lives on in his art and in the moving letters he wrote to family and friends.

VIEW FROM MY WINDOW, ERGANY, 1888
Camille Pissarro, French (1830–1903), oil on canvas, 25⅛" x 31½"

Like many artists of his generation, Camille Pissarro appreciated Japanese landscape paintings. Ike No Taiga, who lived one hundred years earlier, suggested the fields in this painting with an abstract pattern of brushstrokes.

In the 1870s, Camille Pissarro, the great landscape painter, became friend and adviser to Paul Cézanne and Claude Monet. He encouraged the younger artists to pursue their ideas about painting, despite harsh public criticism. When Pissarro was fifty-five years old, he met Georges Seurat and Paul Signac, who were in their early twenties. Their new pointillist technique gave Pissarro a fresh source of energy for his work.

Like Signac and Seurat, Pissarro painted individual dots of color to create the luminous effects of natural light. By placing two colors next to each other on the canvas, instead of mixing paint on the palette, he created the effect of a third color; to the viewer, the colors seemed to blend together. For example, dots of red and yellow produce the color orange when seen from a few feet away.

In this joyous landscape, Pissarro expresses his renewal as an artist and his deep appreciation of rural life. Pissarro shaped this composition to keep our eyes moving in a circular path through the painting. The bright red barn roof points to a stand of poplar trees in the background. A ring of fruit trees around the oval meadow brings our eyes back to the greenhouse, the garden, and Mme. Pissarro in the foreground.

We can see that by using the pointillist technique, Pissarro created the effect of a rainbow of color. But this time-consuming technique slowed down the aging master's productivity. In 1890, he resumed painting in the style that had brought him great fame twenty years earlier.

BIBEMUS QUARRY, about 1895
Paul Cézanne, French (1839–1906), oil on canvas, 25⅝" x 39⅜"

Because he was absorbed in the study of nature, Paul Cézanne isolated himself in the south of France, away from his fellow artists in Paris. The unique way in which he depicted light and space inspired younger artists, such as Henri Matisse and André Derain, who searched for ways to express their artistic vision. To them, Cézanne's lonely search for perfection was heroic.

In an abandoned quarry near Aix-en-Provence, Cézanne studied and painted the huge, jagged rocks that had been carved into a jumble of colliding forms. He shaped this dramatic composition through the contrast of sizes, shapes, and angles. Cézanne rearranged the geometric rock formations in a subtle pattern that leads our eyes on a circular path through the picture.

Large angled blocks of stone on the left and right guide our eyes into the painting. The horizontal shelf in the middle leans toward a wedge-shaped outcrop that sweeps upward. Soft green foliage creeps up the rocky slope to a tree that curves above the horizon, to the right. Here, the diagonal trunk of a tree cut off by the edge of the painting takes us back down along sharply tilted, steplike rocks to the middle of the picture. The arched boulders below shift our attention back into the painting.

Every stroke of Cézanne's brush creates the effect of solidity and light. The enlarged detail (below) shows that he painted patches of red, brown, orange, and gray side by side. Cézanne worked these "constructive touches" at the same angle as the tilted rock to shape the massive stone blocks. With short angled brushstrokes, in many shades of grayish blue, he created weightless clouds in the hazy-looking sky.

In this painting, Paul Cézanne emphasized the steep terrain through the contrast of light tones in the foreground with dark tones in the trees and sky.

28

BEECH FOREST I, 1902
Gustav Klimt, Austrian (1862–1918), oil on canvas, 39⅜" x 39⅜"

Gustav Klimt became a well-known painter at the age of twenty, when he was still a student. After joining the only official art organization in Vienna, Austria, he fought for freedom of expression. The organization was run by old-fashioned people who were more interested in selling works of art than in searching for new ways of painting. In 1897, Klimt formed a new art association that promoted artistic freedom through exhibitions and a monthly magazine.

Important mural and portrait commissions as well as his work for the art association left Klimt with little spare time. But every fall, he left Vienna for the lake district near Salzburg, where he experimented with new ideas by painting landscapes.

For this haunting forest scene, Klimt was inspired by a technique he had observed in Japanese art—he placed the line of the horizon close to the top of the painting to indicate its distance from the viewer. The bird's-eye view and pale gray color in the background suggest depth. The multicolor pattern of individual brush marks on the leaves and speckled tree trunks make this painting seem flat, like a tapestry. With speckles of brilliant gold sunlight that form a strong contrast to the gray and rust tones in the painting, Klimt created a decorative effect.

The year after Klimt painted this ghostly landscape, a mural he created for Vienna's new university was rejected by the head of the school, who thought it was obscene. After this, Klimt refused projects for public buildings and, instead, spent more of his time on landscape painting.

BANKS OF THE BIEVRE NEAR BICETRE, 1904
Henri Rousseau, French (1844–1910), oil on canvas, 21½" x 18"

Before he became a full-time artist, Henri Rousseau had the perfect job for a weekend painter. As a clerk for the customs department, Rousseau worked outdoors, inspecting cargo on river barges in the Paris suburbs. He enjoyed observing the light and the changing seasons, and he often returned to this region to paint after quitting his job.

Tiny figures in their Sunday best make the trees seem enormous by comparison. Rousseau, known for his jungle images, painted tropical foliage on these Parisian trees.

Rousseau was a self-taught artist who learned by making copies of masterpieces in the Louvre museum rather than by attending an art school. At the museum, he developed his technical skills and sharpened his talent for using color. Rousseau painted in a clear, simple style that he believed was the truest—and the best—expression of his feelings about nature.

In this intimate landscape, Rousseau created the illusion of depth by using angles that guide our eyes from the foreground to the background. Four paths, separated by ribbons of grass, sweep back into the distance. A tiny family strolls down the wedge-shaped paths toward the little white house beyond. The banks of a river form another angled shape that points to a red-roofed house and an aqueduct near the horizon.

Rousseau used a narrow range of colors to capture the dreamlike atmosphere of a hazy spring day. He repeated the muted green of the grass in the trees and suggested leafy foliage by painting distinct speckles of yellow ocher on the trees and hedges in the middle. Rousseau framed the scene with towering trees whose swirling branches suggest a spring breeze.

THE CYPRESSES, 1907
André Derain, French (1880–1954), oil on board, 9⁷⁄₁₆" x 13"

In this landscape painting, André Derain honored two master artists who had influenced his work: Vincent van Gogh, for his powerful use of intense colors to express emotion, and Paul Cézanne, for his many paintings of Mont Sainte-Victoire (below). In 1907, Derain spent the summer in the south of France where the two masters had painted. He adopted their themes—the cypresses and the mountain—to create a painting that depicts space and natural light in an entirely different way.

With bold blocks of color, Derain created the impression of depth. Wedge-shaped walls of stone point into the distance. The road, framed by bushy hedges, leads back toward the mountain. Tall greenish black cypresses march into the background. The bright blue pyramid of Sainte-Victoire is mirrored by a pale blue triangle of distant sky.

The intense light of the Provence region inspired Derain's strong colors. For the sky, he painted a shimmering veil of white over cerulean blue. The metallic blue mountain, with its underlayer of reddish lavender, seems to radiate with the heat of reflected light.

In the brilliant southern light, Derain observed that cast shadows were dark reflections of their subjects—not opaque black masses covering other colors. He painted shadows cast by the hedges in the foreground in pale lavender; patches of the same color on the wall at the right indicate shade. The energy with which Derain gave shape to his vision of Mont Sainte-Victoire can be seen in the lively brush marks that animate the surface of this painting.

Paul Cézanne took a distant view of Sainte-Victoire in this oil painting. He defined the massive peak with patches of paint applied with a squared-off brush, creating a textured pattern of brushstrokes.

MOROCCAN LANDSCAPE, 1912
Henri Matisse, French (1869–1954), oil on canvas, 46½" x 31½"

Like an athlete, Henri Matisse did a thorough series of warm-up exercises before starting a large, important painting. Matisse made quick sketches to capture a gesture or a movement and drafted long, detailed studies to explore the complex arrangement of the painting. As he drew, he made decisions as to how he would use lines, colors, and shapes. When he began to paint, Matisse could rely on his instincts, and he used color to express an emotion rather than to describe the actual appearance of things.

On a visit to Tangier, Morocco, in 1912, Matisse found an exotic country with extravagant gardens that delighted his senses. In this painting, Matisse simplified the forms and colors of the lush landscape into his dream of a subtropical paradise.

Matisse drew many studies of acanthus leaves, memorizing their form with both his eyes and his hands. When he painted the acanthus, he simplified the contours and arrangement of the leaves to create a graceful pattern in the foreground. Matisse balanced the curved and flowing arabesque forms of leaves and branches with one stately tree. This strong vertical form creates a striking contrast to the rhythmic pattern of foliage around it.

To convey the warmth of Morocco, Matisse painted a radiant pink over the entire canvas. He covered the foreground with ultramarine to suggest shade. Patches of pink show through the blue to indicate sunlight filtering through the trees. With touches of chrome yellow, Matisse intensified the sensation of heat. The carefully composed balance of pink background and blue foreground and straight and curving lines creates a harmony of color and form.

THE RIDE OF PAUL REVERE, 1931
Grant Wood, American (1892–1942), oil on Masonite, 30" x 40"

"The British are coming! The British are coming!"

Grant Wood was inspired by the story of Paul Revere, the patriot and silversmith who warned his neighbors of the enemy's advance on Lexington and Concord during the American Revolution. Wood believed that ordinary people shaped important events, and he often depicted the everyday life of the farmers in Iowa, where he lived. Wood relocated Paul Revere's historic ride from Massachusetts, where it actually took place, to the midwestern plains, transforming the distant national hero into a hero of Wood's own region.

This precisely painted bird's-eye view has an air of unreality—it looks like a stage set seen from high up in the balcony. Like a theater director, Wood creates special effects, pouring artificial-looking moonlight over the scene from above. He emphasizes the church with a long, sharply defined shadow and casts an eerie neon green glow over the banks of the little stream. Wood painted the geometric forms in precise detail, from the bricks and mortar of the chimneys in the foreground to the round trees in the distance.

Wood reshaped the New England landscape to resemble Iowa, emphasizing the rolling hills with a curving road. He exaggerated reality to create an imaginative and dreamlike impression of a crucial moment in American history. By placing the tiny horse and rider next to the tallest structure, he emphasizes Paul Revere's heroic, solitary role, just as the great American poet Ralph Waldo Emerson immortalized the farmer of the American Revolution who "fired the shot heard round the world."

Grant Wood admired the colors and the precisely detailed foliage in Joachim Patinir's landscapes.

38

RANDEGG IN THE SNOW, WITH RAVENS, 1935
Otto Dix, German (1891–1969), mixed media on pressed fiberboard, 31½" x 27½"

When Adolf Hitler came to power in Germany in 1933, he forced artists to create romantic paintings that would glorify the crazed ideals of Nazi superiority. Otto Dix's paintings, fiercely critical of conditions in Germany, were labeled "perverted" and "immoral." He was fired from his teaching job at the Dresden Academy, and much of his work was destroyed by the Nazis. Fearing for his family's safety, Dix moved with them to the remote village of Randegg.

Although Dix refused to paint the kind of pictures demanded by Hitler—romantic landscapes that expressed the grandeur of nature and, therefore, Nazi

Many twentieth-century painters were influenced by wood-block prints depicting the various moods of the four seasons created by the Japanese artist Andō Hiroshige in the nineteenth century.

glory—he had to sell paintings to support his family. Like Brueghel, a painter admired by Hitler, Dix created a winter scene and chose a view from high above a village. But, he tricked the Nazis with this landscape painting that expresses his own artistic vision and a mood very different from that of Brueghel.

Dix created the atmosphere of a private world shut off from trouble. He warmed the foggy light with a hidden sun. He placed the rust and ocher cottages close together to suggest a cozy mood. But the ancient gnarled tree and the black ravens suggest his great sadness and his isolation from friends in Dresden.

The precision of Dix's brushwork echoes that of another great German artist, Albrecht Dürer. With fine brushes, Dix shaped nearly every feather on the swooping ravens, every branch, and every icicle. Dix borrowed the themes and techniques of past artists in order to create paintings that would sell during desperate times.

41

GRAY HILLS, 1942
Georgia O'Keeffe, American (1887–1986), oil on canvas, 24" x 36"

On her first visit to New Mexico, in 1929, Georgia O'Keeffe was captivated by a desert landscape with dramatic skies that bathed the stark mountains with intense, unfamiliar colors. Nearly every year thereafter, she escaped the frantic pace of New York in the solitude of Ghost Ranch. There she found inspiration for her unique portrayal of landscapes unmarked by human activity.

O'Keeffe often camped out in Navaho territory, near a barren range of hills that she said looked like miles of elephants. Rising before dawn, O'Keeffe observed the play of ghostly moonlight on the massive, creased hills. She created a powerful image that defies our sense of scale: because there are no human figures in this painting, we cannot "measure" the mountain's height.

By eliminating both the background and the foreground, O'Keeffe forms a close-up view that crowds the viewer out of the scene. A narrow slice of icy blue sky, in contrast to the warm black folds of the hills, makes the looming mass appear to come forward. With nearly abstract brush marks that form a strong contrast to the precisely painted rocks, O'Keeffe suggests a few scrubby bushes.

To capture the ghostly quality of fading moonlight, O'Keeffe painted gray highlights that are not much brighter than the shadows. She shaped the mountain's creased flanks with warm shadows that she created by mixing the earth colors—sand, yellow ocher, red— with black and white.

In a long career that ended with her death at the age of ninety-nine, Georgia O'Keeffe created a form of landscape painting that expresses her unique vision of nature's monuments.

The contemporary American artist Yuko Nii created a haunting view of Egyptian dunes in a painting style so realistic that it could almost be mistaken for a photograph.

LYNX WOODS, 1947

Charles Burchfield, American (1893–1967), watercolor on paper laid down on board, 32¾" x 39½"

*F*rom the time he was a child, Charles Burchfield took solitary walks in the forest. He observed the flickering patterns of light and the shapes of windswept leaves; he smelled the musty odor of dried moss and listened to the sounds of forest creatures. Burchfield often lay down in the woods with his eyes closed to feel the energy of the season—he "saw" nature with all of his senses, and to him, even a falling leaf created a sound.

In *Lynx Woods*, Burchfield captured the haunting mood of Indian summer with boldly patterned colors and shapes. With yellow, gray, and umber brushstrokes, Burchfield created a shower of falling leaves. A misty white light in the background gives a sense of depth, inviting us into the woods. But the birch and the pine in the foreground seem to issue a warning. Dusk is approaching, winter is coming, and the forest will soon be dark and cold.

Although he attended art school, Charles Burchfield was chiefly a self-taught artist. Working alone, he developed a unique method of watercolor painting using both transparent and opaque paints, sometimes blending them together to speed the drying time. With transparent yellow, he created streamers of sunlight. Large areas of cool gray and umber make the yellow seem even more brilliant by contrast. On the tree trunks and on the ground, Burchfield created a pattern of yellow and gray "wildcat" markings.

Burchfield rarely traveled; in the forest near his home outside of Albany, New York, he found all that he needed to express his intensely personal view of nature.

Glossary and Index

PAINT: Artists have used different kinds of paint, depending on the materials that were available to them and the effects they wished to produce in their work. Different kinds of paint are similar in the way they are made.

1. Paint is made by combining finely powdered pigment with a vehicle. A vehicle is a fluid that evenly disperses the color. The kind of vehicle used sometimes gives the paint its name, for example: oil paint. Pigment is the raw material that gives paint its color. Pigments can be made from natural minerals and from artificial chemical compounds.

2. Paint is made thinner or thicker with a substance called a medium, which can produce a consistency like that of water or mayonnaise or peanut butter.

3. A solvent must be used by the painter to clean the paint from brushes, tools, and the hands. The solvent must be appropriate for the composition of the paint.

OIL PAINT, 10, 16, 18, 20, 22, 24, 26, 28, 30, 32, 34, 36, 38, 42: Pigment is combined with an oil vehicle (usually linseed or poppy oil). The medium chosen by most artists is linseed oil. The solvent is turpentine. Oil paint dries slowly, which enables the artist to work on a painting for a long time. Some painters add other materials, such as pumice powder or marble dust, to produce thick layers of color. Oil paint is never mixed with water. Oil paint has been used since the fifteenth century. Until the early nineteenth century, artists or their assistants ground the pigment and combined the ingredients of paint in their studios. When the flexible tin tube (like a toothpaste tube) was invented in 1840, paint made by art suppliers became available.

WATERCOLOR, 12, 44: Pigment is combined with gum arabic, a water-based vehicle. Water is both the medium and the solvent. Watercolor paint now comes ready to use in tubes (moist) or in cakes (dry). Watercolor paint is thinned with water, and areas of paper are often left uncovered to produce highlights.

Gouache is an opaque form of watercolor, which is also called tempera or body color.

Watercolor paint was first used 37,000 years ago by cave dwellers who created the first wall paintings.

PERSPECTIVE, 8, 12: Perspective is a method of representing people, places, and things in a painting or drawing to make them appear solid or three-dimensional rather than flat. Six basic rules of perspective are used in Western art.

1. People in a painting appear larger when near and gradually become smaller as they get farther away.

2. People in the foreground overlap people or objects behind them.

3. People become closer together as they get farther away.

4. People in the distance are closer to the top of the picture than those in the foreground.

5. Colors are brighter and shadows are stronger in the foreground. Colors and shadows are paler and softer in the background. This technique is often called *atmospheric perspective.*

6. Lines that, in real life, are parallel (such as the line of a ceiling and the line of a floor) are drawn at an angle, and the lines meet at the *"horizon line,"* which represents the eye level of the artist and the viewer.

In addition, a special technique of perspective, called *foreshortening,* is used to compensate for distortion in figures and objects painted on a flat surface. For example, an artist will paint the hand of an outstretched arm—which is closest to the viewer—larger than it is in proportion to the arm, which becomes smaller as it recedes toward the shoulder. This correction, necessary in a picture using perspective, is automatically made by the human eye observing a scene in life. *Foreshortening* refers to the representation of figures or objects, whereas *perspective* refers to the representation of a scene or a space.

Painters have used these methods to depict objects in space since the fifteenth century. But many twentieth-century artists choose not to use perspective. An artist might emphasize colors, lines, or shapes to express an idea, instead of showing people or objects in a realistic space.

POINTILLISM, 24, 26: To paint with individual dots of color rather than brushstrokes.

PRINT, 40: One of many images created by mechanical means from the same original. Prints can be made from a metal plate (etching, aquatint, engraving), from a block of wood (wood engraving, wood-block print), from a silk gauze (silk-screen print), or from a stone (lithograph).

SCALE, 42: The relationship of the size of an object to that of a human figure. For example: in a painting that depicts a mountain, we can judge the mountain's size only if we compare it to that of a human figure.

TONE, 14, 30: The sensation of an overall coloration in a painting. For example, an artist might begin by painting the entire picture in shades of greenish gray. After more colors are applied using transparent glazes, shadows, and highlights, the mass of greenish gray color underneath will show through and create an even tone, or "tonal harmony." *See also* COLOR

TRANSPARENT, 8, 12, 44: Allowing light to pass through so colors underneath can be seen. (The opposite of OPAQUE.)

TROMPE L'OEIL, 8: A technique used to paint a scene so realistically that the viewer may be tricked into thinking that people and objects in the picture are real—that the flat surface of the painting is a real space. In sixteenth- and seventeenth-century Italian art, this technique was often used to create the illusion of soaring domes and arches in rooms with flat ceilings. *See also* PERSPECTIVE

Credits